Something Yet to Be Named

Something Yet to Be Named

Poems by

Kersten Christianson

Kelsay Books

Cover:
Full Moon on Windy Arm
16" x 16" - oil on canvas
by Daphne Mennell
www.daphnemennellyukonart.com

ISBN: 13-978-1-945752-75-9

Kelsay Books
Aldrich Press
www.kelsaybooks.com

For Bruce and Rie

Acknowledgments

I have so much gratitude to wise teachers and mentors along my MFA/Creative Writing path: Poet Elizabeth Bradfield, Poet Zack Rogow, and Poet Anne Caston. Thank you each and all for indulging my northern inclinations while expanding my literary geographies. To my fellow poet colleagues and friends, the workshop table was all the more productive through your honest, constructive feedback and support.

To Vivian Faith Prescott for the invite to Blue Canoe Writers, a return trip to Wrangell, Alaska, and a spring jar of Spruce Tip Honey.

And to Bruce. You and Rie gave me the gift of time and space to unpack these words. No, the poems do not rhyme. Yes, all the books will venture north again. Thank you for seeing me through to this end, and beginning.

Thank you to the following journals and anthologies for previously publishing the following poems included in this collection, some in earlier draft forms:

Cirque — The Fortymile [You Are Gone Again to the Fortymile]; North Again; Poet Passes: Leaves Words Behind [Elegy]; 9 Kinds of Cottongrass; Visiting the Cabin of *Winter News* above the Tanana River; The Saltbox on Gibson Place; Hometown; Goose & Grove

Connotations — Fiddleheads [9:05 and the sun]

Fredericksburg Literary & Art Review — Rain Down the Mountain; On a Sandbank on Willow Creek They Find Your Body

Halcyon Days — Tonight

Heartbeat: A Literary Journal — Talisman

Icarus Anthology — December 30th; You Know You Walk in Bear Country; Carol's Laminaria

Inklette — New Moon; Inventory, Wrangell, Alaska, 1979

Island Institute — Chicken Bear

Midnight Circus — In the Absence of Sun; Dragons Inspire Fear; The second the rain turned to snow

Mused — Shelter; Flight; Stranding

On the Rusk — This Day; Poetry & Wind; Moon

Peeking Cat Poetry — Free Spirit

Pure Slush — This Is Barrow, But It's Not My Photo; Middle Earth Café: Nakusp, B.C.

Sheila-Na-Gig Online — At the Southern End of Lynn Canal

The Yellow Chair Review — Aunt

Tidal Echoes — In Eliason Harbor; Querencia; Laminaria

Trailer Park Review — Elixir

Venus Magazine — Sound; Light Catcher; Instead, a Sign

We'Moon — From One Good Year to the Beginning of Another

Yellow Medicine Review — My Daughter Teaches Me to Read a Poem

Young Ravens Literary Review — The Port au Port Peninsula; Where Celsius & Fahrenheit Meet

Contents

This Is Barrow, But It's Not My Photo

I.

II.

This Is Barrow, But It's Not My Photo

I could be the tall gal
leaning over your shoulder,
taking in the 10 pm sunset view
through the wild fur ruff of your thick parka;
I've always had a thing for cold weather gear.

Or I could be the girl on Honda,
revving across an icebound lagoon,
trekking along coastline
in the jagged shadow of pressure ridges.

This world is aglow in orange,
a frozen *l'orangerie*, like the one in Paris
only less famous, and older;
timeless like sea and ice.
There's no Monet here, no gilded water lilies;

only, the breath of Bowhead,
the whoosh of snowy owl wings,
the keen of wind,
scampering fox and giggling child.

This is Barrow, but it's not
my photo, and that is not you,
but it could be as I
inch closer to you, my steady windbreak.
This breath working that ruff,

while the light of the sun washes over us.

I.

Family Alder

*From the FS/USDA: Prolific in the Tongass, red alder, **alnus rubra,** produces fruit resembling small pinecones. Its seed is comprised of tiny, dry nutlets with narrow wings.*

Clam nectar brewers, martini drinkers,
halibut and venison eaters

Sharon & Greg, Norma & Paul, Nancy
& the dead grandfather I never knew

The high bank on the Washington side
of the Columbia River to Baranof Island

In the shadow of Verstovia, Arrowhead,
and Mt. Edgecumbe, the dormant volcano
eight miles out

A clam purse of sarcasm, sensitivity, humor;
the lost playground marbles of my childhood:
aggies, cat's eyes, steelies and shooters

Logging, another year at the pulp mill before
closing, fish ladder construction, river bed
restoration, cancer

The wood stacking conversation:
"You can wish in one hand…"

Brief childhood stint at the Presbyterian
church, collection money pooled for candy:
Snickers bars and Nerds

The yellow-green banana seat bike,
the three shades of red-orange 1969 Volkswagen
bug, the ice-skating pond in the muskeg

From brown bears, harbor seal and tidal zones,
northern lights and moon over Kruzof Island

Transplanted purple-crowned rhododendron
starts, forest stands of yellow cedar, fat thumb-digit
raspberries and Sitka spruce

From Fleetwood Mac, Elton John and one-hit
wonders — always a book in hand, Shel
Silverstein to Judy Blume

Through the alder canopy, mountain
over my shoulder, my own kind of quiet sidles
the sea, wraps the summit like mist

Three Tanka: Traveling the Yukon
to Southeast Alaska

Klondike summer crowd:
geeks, drifters, Deutsche tourists.
Dawson rain, dry tent.
Our Yukon joy: booze red wine
with me under a blue tarp.

      *

Cloudy green waters
meet black in the shadow of
a southbound ferry.
Here, a smack of jellyfish —
clench & release of ocean moons.

      *

Home, slow boat's return.
The morning sun, a surprise.
Broken scud, wispy,
light steps through spruce & cedar:
shuffle and drum of branches.

Our Northern Text

Three dancing leaves remain today
on the Japanese maple outside the window,
scarlet spinners flit in coastal rain and frenzied wind.
The empty bird feeder, metal trim and glass pane,
clangs its memory chant against the trunk.

And you, with laughing eyes, full beard and holey shirts,
stand perched alongside muddy, raised road,
somewhere near Jack Wade Creek, years ago,
our lives' ephemera bundled up in burgeoning blue tarp and rope,
mostly books and a mug or two.

It did not matter that the tire would go flat,
we'd ride the Top of the World on a narrow spare,
that we'd never been to Dawson,
or that we might miss the ferry out of Haines.

The Bunkhouse offered solace and warm wool blankets,
the Pit, good drink and a few tunes,
to the backdrop of the roiling Yukon —
our new chapter.

Light the candle again,
these days of green needle
and patchy orange foliage
dip into the sea.

Middle Earth Café: Nakusp, B.C.

It's a muggy, summer day here
wood trim like dark ale
contrasts with perky raspberry-hued
carnations in pottery vases on each table.

Blank note cards in altered boxes, photographed
and bejeweled, sit out on the counter,
Mandala Moon Divine Arts.
The magic of the Kootenay.

A postcard stamped *New Zealand* boasts
Frodo and Samwise in capes and smiles.
Altars of wood and stone appear
in random corners of the café.
Stained glass moons and World Tree
adorn the windows, along with a sign,
a reminder to be kind:

Don't piss off the fairies.

North to Kluane: Three Guardsmen Lake

after W.S. Merwin

Winds unharnessed,
the lake ripples and strains against its borders,
stretches and unfurls along banks of wild grass,
spills to streams trickling over stone.

Once three guardsmen stood
vigil here, here above this empty road,
viewing lone swans adrift on the lake.
Once, three guardsmen
crested the hill, thinking
of warmth and a woman
who walked the edge of water
into autumn and the coming cold.

And now, these wandering sentinels:
red-throated loons, snow buntings,
ptarmigan.

The Forest Lives in Nanaimo

Just south of Nanaimo is the Living Forest Campground.
We groaned at the name, surely a spin-off of wilderness
    for yuppies.
Even the way hipper, cool Canadian guy at the bike shop
    in Victoria asked, "Aren't all forests living?"
But we fell asleep the first night under its verdant canopy
    to the honks of Canadian geese in the green estuary
    and the ferries traversing travelers from island
    to smaller island to mainland.
Meandering pilings litter the tidelands.
Celestine sky matches the crystal adorning
    the picnic table - a gift from Bruce from Mazilli's
    Rocks, the rock shop in old town.
Smoke from the Lillooet fires mutes the sky —
    sun blazes distant windows red and warms beach logs.
A lone seal breaststrokes up the channel while a caterpillar
    inches across the tent screen.

The Port Au Port Peninsula

This far shore measures
the cadence of old French and Basque languages,

the first notes of a fiddle removed from a battered case;
the old songs and stories of fine catch and shipwrecks
around crackling bonfire;
perhaps even the laughter of a little girl
who disappeared into the rock,
into the sea.

We gather fossilized rocks
imprinted with the signatures of trilobites.

There is wave-battered wood broken from lobster pots,
knotted rope, and broken shells
to haul home for winter beading projects.

This far shore keeps the beat of my heart.

In the Absence of Sun

Barrow, Alaska, Latitude 71° north, late November

It's 30 below now and we
have kissed daylight goodbye, surrendered
to darkness, 24-hour moon, trudged
our way to school, past *Stuaqpaq* the grocery store,
which sounds like "Snack Pack": $10 a gallon for milk.
Fresh vegetables. Snow machines. In hiking boots,
black Gator masks, odd-looking fleece hats,
our exposed skin cries out for warmth.

Paused here between the stairs of the Alaska
Commercial Company store and Cab Alley
in the vacuum of North wind, I hear —
above murmuring motors of early morning
vehicles and the hum of the building —
snow.

A squall of iced white chips, frozen glitter, pecks
against the glass of a windshield, tatters
against the steel of a Quonset hut in its downward spiral,
cartwheeling across the North Slope.

9:05 and the Sun

shimmies behind the volcano,
dipping below the horizon.
Children scamper home,
shrieking their delight
to the sun god who sent
good weather this day.

58 degrees. Warmth
we've not had since fall,
piercing sun greening the bare branches,
shimmering the sea.

Like fiddleheads we stay out
late - unfurling our winter bones.
Root-bound and hearty, we stretch —
east to west — from break of day
to alpenglow. We come to
late night rest under new moon.

Where Celsius and Fahrenheit Meet

In the outdoor
cold of a frozen street,
dark and empty,
40 below sounds
hollow.

Snow crystals coat the fur
of red fox chasing a red fox
through wind-shifting drifts —
fox trails.

Scampering shadows cast
by streetlight, dim aurora,
and sliver of moon
fade

to gray smoke lifting
from chimneys, our hair
frozen silver, a white thread
of the Yukon.

December 30th

While brewing hot cinnamon tea
I add this page to my book of Alaskan sunsets.
Memories of those in brilliant orange, cast light on Sitka Sound
      through the black outline of bare alder branches.
Others slide behind misshapen forms
      of frozen sea ice, indigo and dark wine skies
      blanket the Bering Sea
      the profiles of Bruce and the dog against coastline
      and horizon.
I've chased the setting sun from Redoubt to Iliamna;
      from Mile 13 of K-Beach Road to Homer,
      one cold dwelling to another,
      for the warm company of sister and friend.

What is more important this day
than to watch golden sun
light its low path across the sky,
illuminate the squalls, and
add shadows to the wind?

While the sun romps between storms
and the skies eventually darken,
my memories travel with the sun
on a vaporous trail of tea.

Dragons Inspire Fear

But not this day — the morning's light,
too brilliant to slay, bounces through sea-facing windows
kindles the amber glass scales

of the beast perched atop the Teen Lit. collection.
It blinks its yellow-red eye, a burning sun,
at the gathering children below.

A shake awakens the residual dust, chatter
of serendipitous celebration — of good fortune, parchment-
printed money and flame, of paper butterflies wavering

to the moon, of red and gold masks, Chinese
zodiacs, paper lanterns in this new
year of the dragon.

You Know You Walk in Bear Country

Off the highway. The dwarf
fireweed are in pre-bloom.
Spruce tips are ripe for picking.
Beard moss shifts, dances.
Scud slips across mountains.

Tumbled garbage cans.
Unexpected rain:
drizzle to downpour to nothing.
Flush of salmonberry blossom.
Skunk cabbage stalks devoured.

Inviting green grasses.
Rusty hinge kelp on beach.
Skittish heron in estuary.
Raucous ravens overhead.
You pack bell, spray, the advisable firearm.

Carol's Laminaria

Luminary,
your flame draws you
to the rocky beach
where the kelp
washes upon the shore:
slick, brown blades coiled
by bull kelp tossed
with popweed.

You carry an armful
of slippery laminaria
to the tree line;
think of women hanging salmon,
while draping your haul
over a branch
to sway,
sing and dry
in the wind.

In photographs
you capture the whorls
and turns of sea
tangle. You leave
behind your beach
finds: smooth stick,
broken shell. I look

for your signature,
your thumbprint,
your gathered kelp
this side of the equinox,
this side of the sea:

gold thread embroidered,
cupping the moisture
of drizzle and herring snow
in March.

Merrill, I Have Made Your Acquaintance

Traversing these park trails, the beaten track,
during off-hours, when all is quiet,
I swear your spirit still roams

here; quiet stride on spruce-needled paths,
treasures — bark, clam shell, raven feather — positioned
on wood benches, a photographer's dream, an artist's haven.

I am left to speculate, explore
vague snippets: musty magazines, out-of-print
books, beach glass among rock.

Note: E.W. Merrill was a turn-of-the-century art photographer in Sitka,
Alaska. He also served as the first official custodian of Sitka National
Historical Park from 1919-1922.

Blackberries in May

It is summer once again,
or at least the first
day of summer for teachers.
Cloudy, gray, 52 degrees
like the last 52 days, but without the rain
and I've given in to giddy.

The first blackberry crop
of the season has arrived.
Blackberries —
bigger than bull kelp,
maybe the size of skunk cabbage tips,
but a bit of joy.

Not Sitka blackberries, but from Mexico,
where it must be summer every day.
Twelve ounces for $5.99,
this taste of summer,
this moment's yearly passage.

This Day

Tie-dye shirts edge the clothesline,
catch the afternoon sea breeze,
dry quickly in this warm, summer sun.
This summer day, this summer
like no other, addles the locals —
supercharges the flora and fauna.

Eugene and Julian swim one day
in mirrored high mountain lakes
and the next in the open sea.
At Old Harbor Books, Liz tells me
of 10-inch banana slugs.
She marvels at the 5-inch pea pod
I've plucked from my parents' garden.

The sun produces
berries like none other,
blue as a storm crossing sea;
red like the spent fireweed glowing
in the orange of sunset.
Huckleberries, blueberries, raspberries
fill the bellies of bears and humans.

Other than the bundled tourists visiting
from the ship of the day, fleece coats and
rain gear hang dry on walled pegs,
bundled in closets, put away
for fall storms.
Until then, berries fill the freezer.
We pretend it is always like this.
We pretend the sun is ours.

Estuary

Clouds shift shape,
bob trees in blustery winds.
Keep the rains at bay.

Bird on the guard
rail, winter sun warms its back;
a deity with wings.

Starrigavan raven,
cocked head and feathers ruffled.
Eye like a glass bead.

Hometown

Shuttered up winter town: rain puddling
in the gutters and cracks, I am the string

of inconsistencies. Twinkle lights;
eight bulbs burned out, half winking

stars flash against the art shop's storm —
dirty windows. Blink of the eye,

the blue of the mailbox gnarled,
twisted by the drunk driver

from the Moose. The Russian curios line
the dusty shelves of the old Random House

gift shop: Lacquer boxes, Fabergé baubles,
matryoshkas, the little nest of dolls (one word

inside another, inside another) in rain gear, dry
boots, an apprentice of joy buoyed

by the crack of flashy January sunlight,
the truth of sky just before the dark.

The Second the Rain Turned to Snow

Making pace down Kogwonton Street past the backside of Kenny's Teriyaki Restaurant and his sweet & sour chicken, not quite to Murray's and a new pair of Xtratuf boots, but definitely beyond the bridge, high above black glass sea, wind-whipped and frenzied, ruffled feathers and foam. On Backstreet, mid-winter is still aglow — tinsel on spruce and Russian Christmas close. Strip down to the woolen layer that gathers snowflakes in its folds; align my breath and stride with gust. I'll not get closer to that cloud-fringed moon and the gauzy stars this night. Here the wind chimes greet me, clang, stretch metal arms as far as their cords allow, and wood smoke curls around us. Sing chimes, for calm sea, full belly, and a long walk tonight in warm boots.

Summit

Supermoon

           ablaze, alpine
      trails beckon.
My journal is open.

Fireweed

          carves out
      an existence even if
among cliff
      and stone.

Like words

          in margin
      it frames
glacier's edge,

ignites

          in summer's sun,
      smolders into winter's
blank-paged

return.

Aunt

Ginny by most, Virginia by my grandmother with the emphasis and drag on "gin." Vir-*gin*-ia married into an old Norwegian Ballard family. We all wore the Norse sweater vests for it, knitted wool and pewter buttons. Grandma Annie, the matriarch, let us cousins race through the house, tumble into the backyard for summer popsicles and sleepovers. It's hot wearing a Norse sweater vest in summer. Every day Ginny played tennis. Classy, impeccable taste, much more a carbon copy of my grandmother than either would care to admit: shopping at Nordstrom's, the click and swish of credit card, the spin cycle of return and exchange for more and new; dinner parties with fine cloth linens and hors d'oeuvres (including either spinach or artichoke); and the wine, always the white wine, propped between the morning Bloody Mary, or mimosa, and the evening bourbon. White wine with ice cream. Vir-*gin*-ia divorced, hooked up with the banker, spent chunks of the year in Hawaii, Arizona, and the Pacific Northwest. She worked as a hospice volunteer. Her laugh was contagious for a long time. She thought Alaska was weird; it may as well have been Siberia. She came up one year to take care of our family. Visited me at college. Helped organize my wedding on a Sitka dock. Met my daughter two cold springs ago. In Mukilteo, she built winter fires in her fireplace with Duraflame Logs from the QFC on 24th Ave NW. Ginny spent the last month potting spring flowers for her balcony: wax begonias and pansies. She visited her favorite restaurants: Anthony's Shilshole for clam chowder, hot sourdough bread and Ray's Boathouse for shrimp Cobb. Returned her unused chemo pills to her doctor. Last weekend the hospice workers moved her bed into the living room, the best view of bloom, Puget Sound and quiet breeze.

Summer's End

In August, the red berries cluster.
A timeless, offbeat drum begins:
salmon slapping the water.

Brown bears are beckoned —
a sow, two cubs, one lone young male —
and all the thrill-seeking humans

who come here too,
who are angling for
the perfect photographic shot

to prop on the bookshelf at home
behind the votive candle
and summer-gathered beach glass.

I'm here too, hard-pressed today,
thinking of the coming change:
quiet days between the winter gales.

Tonight

New Year's Eve in faraway Times Square,
        overrated, surely, with its crowds standing
in a confetti downpour, the cut Waterford crystals reflecting
        hope for wisdom, kindness, gentler times ahead.

Here, the New Year arrives quietly, the wintry
        waters of Sitka Sound drifting on the ebbing
and surging tides under brittle stars and pale light
        of the near full moon.

While a mournful buoy sounds in open sea
        and the branches of alder and cedar shiver,
I light a candle and send it forth — a wish for peace —
        watching it float into the night on twists of wood smoke
from nearby homes, catching the tail of the dim aurora borealis.

Flight

A red-breasted sapsucker
plummets from the morning sky
crash lands
on the cold pavement.

Bill to the ground,
its wings flop,
lift and shroud; a fallen angel
on any good Friday.

Bundle it in your sweater,
threadbare, but warm;
cradle it against your chest,
its breath quiet and still.

You drive to work,
balance bird, bag and coffee
down the sterile hall,
convinced only science
can mend.

Later, you learn,
outstretched wings take flight,
red feathers eclipse sun.
He has risen once again.

Girdwood to Reykjavik

This day of sun,
     mountain
          and sky:

a summer
     bangle, seven
          glaciers,

our daughter
     playing among
          painted chairs.

You are miles away
     on a distant
          island in a far-off sea.

Three days out,
     I write.
          To close the distance.

Tanzanite Dreams

The red carpet unfurls
as the day's flock of tourists
disembarks from the season's big ships.
They flood the Alaskan destination *du jour*,

herd into town, block
the Main Street artery, elbow to elbow the narrow
strip of sidewalk. Made jovial by travel, they
wear plastic ponchos in the rain, balance shopping bags,
forage through stores labeled "locally owned."

Locals dress in costume; gold rush barons
and dance hall girls offer 1898
and Starbucks to go —

even the stately Golden North Hotel
hustles trinkets: plastic totem poles, South
African gemstones, fine imported China,
cheap t-shirts.

Roll up the carpet at the end of the day, the end
of the season. In the creak and sway of weather-
crusted chains holding business placards, listen
to the wind whispering

the stories of those
who have tried their luck here;
buffeting its keen down the couloirs
of blue-lavender mountains.

In truth, who doesn't want to find,
a good deal, to eat the flaked
flesh of salmon, see a bear? Don't
we all want it to never end?

Sad Rubble Not Knowing the Hands of an Artist

Bright sun alights dust-
     shrouded trinkets
     (mask, drum, basket)
          nameless, manufactured

elsewhere. Collateral
     debris ensnared
          in a torn seine net,

adrift and unclaimed.
     Here, the roundabout
          of the summer tourist dollar:

plastic bric-a-brac
     jettisoned into a lead-
          painted sea

     of sameness.

From a Hummock on the Edge of the Great Northern Peninsula

Response to dg nanouk okpik

I skirt along the slabbed coastline pieced like a plaited braid.
You say it's a place of trails
etched by tribolites in mud made stone. We are sojourning,
pursuing empty, ancient worm burrows at the edge
of Port-Aux-Choix, when we catch sight of the five-second
beacon through wind and fog from the Point Riche
pepperpot. Nose to the stone, our yellow lab chases receding
rivulets, crashes headlong into the salty wash of a rolling sea.
We trek the limestone ledges, smooth, wedged plates,
darkened by spray and mist, pocked by chartreuse tidal weed,
through barren's willow, wild chives, woody arnica.
To the gull shriek of the wind, a snowy owl swoops
into the periphery, its white feathers ruffled, outlined
by hazy sun. She blankets the storm with her wings,
offering warmth along the battered shoreline.
With the onset of evening, her tongue claps against her beak:
    Shell of sea urchin, far from home, finding home.

October

From the ink-black sky
she emerges, this moon:

crescent, croissant,
tangerine slice

a mandarin autumn light
patterns

the lacework
of bare alder.

High Wind Watch

I walk the looped park trails,
the uneven lines of millibar
on a map of pending storm.
Searching for squall,
I find the creak and moan
of cedar and spruce,
the routine blast
of whining wind
where river's maw
opens into sea.

All darkening day,
I shuffle papers
at my desk, watch and wait
for its slam into shore,
the shake of the windowpane,
the bombast of alder leaf
and staccato rain
against glass,
through hair.

Blood Moon

To the north, the rubicund moon reaches down,
down to Flat Top.
Her fiery spirit gazes upon snow, stone and ice,
illuminating edges and footholds.
She marks winter's end as we implore the sun's return.
To the south, our view of the ruddy beauty is shrouded
by cloud and rain.

Her fiery spirit kindles crags and peaks.
No late night lunar eclipse to view, just the hush
of a wool blanket.
To the south, night's orb is masked
by cloud and rain.
Her play with shadow treks the summit
of our sleep.

No lunar eclipse to view, we sleep
in the warmth of a quiet house.
To the south, our view of the ruddy beauty is obscured
by cloud and rain.
Shadows trek the summit of our sleep,
and to the north, the rubicund moon reaches down,
down to Flat Top.

Meditation

The trollers return
home to harbor
after chasing their
winter king catch.

A split agate,
this night's sunset;
lavender &
flame. Horizon

casts a defined line
between the water
and wind; catch and
a chance escape.

Hot turkey soup
on the stove, chai
tea in a glazed mug,
I imagine

sodium flare
against salmon scale;
one flip, a banded arc,
the glint before splash.

Harvest

At Cedar Cove
in Katlian Bay
we pull the pots.
Wearing blue
rubber gloves we
pull, hand over hand,
grip the wet line,
haul
against davit.

We pull for
Dungeness crab,
shelled keepers emerge
among moon jelly
bloom: this smack,
this swarm, this cluster.

Outside waters
churn to chop,
the frenetic clashing
of pincers
in bucket,
the warmth
returns to hands,
like crab
cooked in a pot.

Clamming: The Low Tide Trail

Anatomy of a clam: Hinge ligament, gills, adductor muscle, siphon, mantle, muscle, foot.

Clam nectar brewers, your people drink the salty brine
from the bottom of the steamer.

Washington shoreline, hard-packed sand beach, campfire
kindled just inside tree line, a grandma to cup
and warm your cold hands with her own

hands that had wrapped around the handle
and shaft of a shovel, and carried the burden
of mismatched buckets.

Along Alaska shores, a garden shovel breaks through the top
layer of rock, the next, of gravel. Here in the murk, butter clams
drop from their beds. You shovel water against walls,

expose clams, and you pick. You dig and douse
in the circle of a kerosene lantern's muffled hush. Dig
and douse, you pick and drop in the bucket.

You carry your haul of butters to the edge
of the sea smudged by night and rinse
for the next night's chowder.

Clams, clean and mince
Carrot, coin
Onion, skin, layer and dice
Bacon, fry crisp and chop
Evaporated milk, pour and simmer
Knead and knot of crusty bread, slice and butter

Grandfather, the largest clam among the eel-grassed edge:
he is returned to his cavern, as is the smallest of his shelled brood.
Gratitude.

Catch in bucket, light in hand, shovel as walking stick,
you plod your return along the low tide trail: winter moon
and hoarfrost. Beyond the haul, the harvest, full belly —
the silent shuffle of the far-off tide.

Instead, a Sign

11 October 2005

Here on the island, the autumn rains
pound incessantly, winds
shake the shingles, snow dusts
the high peaks of the Sisters
and, in deference to falling leaves,
my dahlias bloom.

Yesterday, wrapped warm
in a purple blanket, sipping
hot cranberry tea, I felt
your first stirrings. I mistook
you for a grumble.

Instead, a sign of life, of spring to come.

II.

Inventory, Wrangell, Alaska, 1979

sea-greens shillying
in the tidal exchange

one tiny eel flipping
a letter "c" in the palm of a child's hand

logs loosened by storms,
freed from rafts, afloat

beach asparagus, bull kelp, ficus
rockweed, black ribbon, sea-lettuce

once-coiled rope segmented
for crab pots, anchor lines, buoys

bottle caps, hermit crabs
scuttling from upturned rocks

pottery shards, beached sea-glass,
marbles: jagged, worn smooth, pitted

broken toys, corroded pennies, lost keys —
no Japanese floats

8,000-year-old petroglyphs, sharp rock, stones
for curve and skip: stacked, grained, metamorphic

stone steps, one upon another, pathways
to and from the shallows of tears

deadheads chain sawed, cut, split,
stacked for firewood

a rusted tangle of bicycles, crippled
chains, reflectors fragmented

one split board swing
hanging from a spruce branch

Mother crying cross-
legged on a mattress she hauled
to the sea-facing window

Goose & Grove

*Upon reading **Song** and **The Orchard***

Oh, Brigit,
your whistling goat head tickles
the edges of my slumber. It severs
my line to childhood as I listen
to its shrill and shaky song,
mingling with the sweetness
of your words.

In the bucolic orchard:
silver lake, doe and fawn, crow,
finch, swan. Apple tree, orange;
the satyr guards the
south gate

where dark madness dwells.
The midwinter madwoman
feeds empty cobs of corn
from a stone bridge to a stream
empty of trout, or koi,
or salmon.

Wander

I.

night and downpour
you cross the bridge
from the empty airport to campus
harbored fishing fleet, glare
of sodium light, flash
and glimmer channel
the low tide
reek

there might be
mountains
you saw them in glossy photos
carved trails from shore to summit
bunchberry, spruce needle, lupine

there might be mountains

II.

how did you compass
your north? carrying
a single duffel, baseball
cap, three holey sweatshirts,
a snuff can's signature
in the back pocket
of worn jeans;

flying into the arc
of a setting sun, a new
narrative, leave behind

the alcoholic father,
the midwestern
plain

III.

there are mountains and inlet
you harvest shrimp, log deep-fathomed
sleep in the bunk of a rocking troller
darkness pierced only by starlight

dreams of silk-tasseled yellow corn
you catalog and consume your catch:
venison, halibut, dolly varden
you shoot hoops, attend
some classes

foxtail, fireweed, willow
in the yukon summer land
you drink molson play
beer-league softball
friends gift you lodging
hand-me-down shirts

IV.

tundra, taiga, arctic slope
bering air drops you
and a gallon of whole milk
36 miles shy of the chukchi peninsula
you tread upon pea gravel
into the *polynya*
the winds that shape ice

six times you purchase
a student's *first* ivory carving
catch a stone
aimed for your knee

you gather shards
of whale bone
the pelt
of an arctic fox
cup wooden trade beads
in the warm palm
of your hand

V.

arc of sundog, of story,
of noontime moon
you bridge the span of tide
the gamut of cloudburst
of drizzle and snow

there might be mountains, might
be a woman with books,
a daughter waiting to be born

Come Closer

As close as you can get
to Bob Dylan in Sitka, on Baranof Island.
Late Friday night, midwinter
warm flannel with a Guinness in hand —
light the candle.

I do recall
that same frothy stout in a chilled pint glass
on the other coast.
A bar in Charlottetown, on Prince Edward Island
        with a shamrock signature inscribed on the head.
Somebody sang Stan Rogers
as closely as they could manage.

From there, home to here,
the full moon is past, the baby sleeps.

View from the Adirondack Chair

                    The alpine meadows
don their summer wear verdant, lush, from this vantage
point at sea-level slopes. Wildflowers
abundant and thriving,
                    the first-year lawn that needs mowing
every third day, long clusters of yellow on the Golden Chain tree,
Scarlet Hawthorn, lemon Columbine, pale-blue masses of fading
forget-me-nots.
                    Imagine a brightly colored Adirondack
Chair — turquoise or tangerine — resting amidst this lush world,
the dogs nearby, the only obstruction of an ocean view
the heavy cedar boughs limbed to the roofline
of the neighbor's guesthouse.

First Hike

We take you, at six weeks of age,
on your first hike, up the winding trail
along Indian River inland from the ocean.

You travel, sound asleep, cushioned
against your Dad's chest,
bear bread on a stout hemlock tree.

Three dogs pound the trail ahead.
Their padded feet weave circles
through the river, into the muskeg.

We trek through budding brush, old growth trees
draped in gauzy beard moss,
and skunk cabbage stalks.

The early anticipation of your spring arrival:
chaotic, conflicted, joyful.
May you always have these trees, coastline, and wooded trails.
Let this day be marked for you.

9 Kinds of Cottongrass

Composed after reading Linda Hogan's collection of poetry, **Dark. Sweet.**

At Haines Junction I arrive
at page 400 and veer south
past Dezadeash Lake,
through the Coast Mountains
and cross the border
for the saltwater of Lynn Canal,
glacier-fed green, and again,
Alaska.

I close the book, look up.

There are no turtles here,
or dancing deer women
in blue and garnet skirts.
There are brown bears,
high peaks, azure broken
by cumulus.

Cottongrass sways in mountain winds.
On his back, a raven carries away
the white clouds.

Visiting the Cabin of *Winter News* above the Tanana River

Like opening the door to my grandfather's greenhouse in South
Seattle, long after he tilled under the raspberry patch,
the cucumbers, the bordering dahlias to make his earth flat.

Even the cherry tree - arms reaching for Mt. Rainier,
for the bright trollius sun, reaching over the fence
into Mrs. Reneker's yard – slashed, cut down and burned.

The grate of a stiff hinge, flutter of a Visqueen flap
covering the broken glass pane, the structure exhaled
its musty breath as I enter the space of the green-thumbed.

Here, the rusted gardening tools: claw,
hoe, and spade. Here, the boxes of fertilizer; hard-
packed, the tops coated with dust.

I don't know, as he did, the wisdom of planting
seeds by moonlight, or of following the dog-
eared pages of the Farmer's Almanac,

but I have walked now the straight
rows of his garden; I have caught the season's fat
berries dropping from the vine, the words

lingering in these empty places.

Fire Ban Along the B.C. Coastline: Salt Spring

It's 80 degrees, unheard of by locals,
    celebrated nonetheless.

We arrive to dry gardens, blooming prisms,
    even the weeds are parched,

a blue Volkswagen bug parked in a rhododendron.
    Green turtles swim the perimeter of their lake.

The coffee is strong and organic.
    We've acquired a new tablecloth —

a sarong of Celtic knot pattern and tie-dye.
    Bruce photographs blue dragonflies.

Rie dreams of indigo
    waters and fairy princesses.

Free Spirit

On the first day of spring that feels like spring,
and in spite of the morning's tiny snowflakes
        flying by in the breeze —
        airy sparkles, Friday magic —
the girl spends the afternoon in the sun.
She wears her funny short pants, a blooming
        garden of movement and color,
        white socks pulled up to her shins,
        her magenta fleece jacket zipped to her neck
        to cut the chill of the wind.
She darts between activities:
        chasing, dragging, carrying the cat;
        sweeping spirals in the winter dust
        of the cul-de-sac with her mini witch broom;
        riding her training-wheeled bike in loopy circles,
        ever more daring, leaning far right then left.

Sun

Occasionally she opens
the blinds, to remind me she is there.

She dusts the glass-beaded
baubles swinging in the windows.

She washes in gold light
my bookshelves, my desk,

the dust collected in the corners,
the spider plant drooping on the sill.

She goes on about her day,
moving across hushed waters,

gliding silently back into the wine-dark sea.

Words

The rare 80 degrees in Sitka today has
eclipsed the dreary drone of summer rains.
We are girls of the sun and the rain,
you proclaim as you skip down the forest path.

You babble with ravens in the canopy
and name each slug *Baby*.
You pocket coins at the Money Bear
and other treasures:
        eagle feather, blue bead, lichen.

Near the end, we quicken our pace,
avoid the busloads of visitors.
Not even this alters your song.

Three years old and full of spontaneous
song that could be poetry — if I just understood your words.

Talisman

for Bruce

I want to tell you
    about the tooth
        Rie pulled:

copper penny wedged
    in the rough tread
        of a rubber brown boot;
remaining seed
    in the bottom
        of the popcorn bowl;
Smooth pebble in sand,
    good luck quartz found
        on John Brown beach.
Once you ran your finger —
    torn and roughened by halibut
        hooks — over her bumpy baby gums.
If I handed you this tooth,
    would you marvel
        in its wholeness and loss.

Where are you?

Eliason Harbor

Potted nasturtia flame on the stern
deck of the old tug, *Adak*, apricot and saffron
lingering as the haul fades summer into fall.

My daughter has gifted them, these florets, these
love tokens from an eight-year-old, sliding
from her hair, scrunched in her pockets.

Maybe this is what can still be learned: how
to face the sea, blazing the margins with color,
adorned in garlands of vermillion and marigold, how

to send wispy runners into the cold unknown.

Sitka

Shimmery sea foam —
herring frolic in the tide.
Mournful buoy moans.

                    *

Fat salmonberries
dripping from limber branches —
dark raven's breakfast.

                    *

Chilly, damp, worn wool
wet on the fisherman's back.
Say goodbye, tourist.

                    *

Mountains meet ocean.
Trails quiet through Totem Park —
leafless alders dance.

Poetry & Wind

I rise early
in a quiet house
under the dark sky
to tend dogs and savor
the morning's coffee;
bitter-tinged and hot.

Consider
the shape of a stanza
across this blank paper page;
words of precision
and balm.

Even the ravens
are silent this morning.
Their shapes
hidden among branches
feathers ruffled
to house warmth.

The house is still.
Warm Taku winds,
clatter and chime in the alder,
crack against my window.
Still coffee cools.
Still the page waits.

Moon

My Facebook feed is filled this week
with full moon images,
the news of a weekend lunar eclipse.

I'm never quite certain
what time these events actually occur —
you know, an eclipse in Alaska time and all —

but in the circle
of my cast iron griddle
bubbles the first crêpe of the morning.

Like a Jesus image
imprinted on the heel of sliced bread,
this thin, gauzy pancake sports a crescent moon

in its cooked, cratered surface.
Valleys and peaks catch
the dip and lilt of my daughter's questions:

> *Mama, is this your grandma's recipe?*
> *Mama, was your grandma Danish?*
> *Mama, is this Grandma Sharon's recipe?*
> *Mama, did she find the recipe from the Internet?*

The recipe is ours.
Moon in my kitchen, lineage
by crater; it is the one thing I know well.

Berry Picking

Through the bramble
into the salmonberry patch.

Past the pink bloom,
the smattering of new trifoliates.

Before the bare stalk of winter
arrives: sharp thorn, skin-splitting.

Sun plays on foliage.
Shadows fidget.

Fat berries dangle
from the branch.

Press their juicy ripeness
onto this page.

Chicken Bear

Through the flick of rain-slickened branch, rattle
and shake of Indian Celery seeds, you crash
and blunder

in the gloom. You stalk the backyard
fowl, skirt the Cross Trail easement
through felled alder leaves.

Never mind the natal
stream: a pulsing vein, the flip and slap
of leaping salmon — a wild heart —

you run amok with wild abandon.
With a beast in the forest,
we are all savage children.

Yukon Sojourn

To the East a forest fire blazes in its early stages,
far below the clear Klondike and muddy Yukon converge.
Rickety Dawson buildings slant haphazardly,
crooked teeth adorned with lively names:
      Bombay Peggy's, the Westminster, the Bunkhouse;
          lilac & amber,
          apricot & blue.

Pierre Burton, Robert Service, Jack London —
      all penned a few verses in this town.
The Palace Grand Theater, even after reconstruction, remembers her
dance hall girls.
Old Crow to the North; Whitehorse to the South,
The afternoon cloud cover offers interlude from the sun.

Promises of gold whisper through the wispy tips of Fox Tail
      while Rie plays in the grass.
French bread and Havarti, we picnic
on the Dome high above Dawson City.
The miles between here and home:
      Wilderness,
          Fireweed,
              Saltwater.

North Again

rare peppered gem
this tangerine moon
a slice of blood orange

my love and I
without daughter or dogs
we navigate dark sky

by snowpack and stars
follow bermed icy roads
sidle the Yukon River

mantled spruce, fir, pine —
frivolous tendrils writhe
across lonely road

wrap the paws of lynx
plodding west into the wind
we circle back

south to the sea
find a red moon of sea glass
lucky penny, stone cairn, rusty key

Light Catcher

Like the light catcher
in my window,
I want to string
this day, catch & hang it
in the sun.
Swarovski crystals
of blue heron backs,
red berried clusters
perched atop Devil's Club,
verdant beard moss —
the old lace
in spruce branches.
To catch the light,
add argent spacers —
aluminum boats,
silver flashers
chasing coho
salmon,
mixed with
purple mussel shells,
orange kelp
stitching the tide line,
bone, vertebrae
of salmon carcass
litter the river's
mouth,
the clear droplets
of this week's
strands of rain,
crackled glass
yellow, August sun.
Knot both ends.

Eye hook, strand
of beads, sun catcher,
prism caster;
I want to string
this day, hang it
in my window.

At the Solstice

A ghost-white salmon sits in my windowsill.
Today we'll paint with splashy acrylics: lime, copper, and magenta
On a porch warmed by full afternoon sun.
Salmon in the trees.

Today we'll paint with splashy acrylics: lime, copper, and magenta.
It's not your traditional Alaskan salmon.
Salmon in the trees,
A fish out of water without wings —

it's not your traditional Alaskan salmon,
This ghost-white, plywood salmon.
A fish out of water without wings
Sporting kaleidoscopic color: Orange, violet, and aqua.

This ghost-white, plywood salmon,
Will it dance in the trees of Totem Park —
Flash orange, violet, and aqua —
This ghost-white salmon in my windowsill?

You Are Gone Again to the Fortymile

The Fortymile is a mining region where eastern interior Alaska meets the Yukon Territory.

Damn your northern adventures
staking their claim on you
yet another summer.

Rie and I celebrate little moments:
      lawn sprinkler use in a rainforest,
      brown bear at Starrigavan Estuary,
      early blueberries.

Rie names you, and boats, and ravens.
She fist-picks forget-me-nots
and scribbles chalk drawings
on the trunk of the Japanese maple;
they could be runes.

Somewhere in there
is her own explanation of your absence.

I tell her stories of your past life as a cartographer,
your simple tools: compass, fine pen, North Star -
of little consequence to a toddler.
We greet the few ferries to the island.
Eventually one will carry you home.

Today

Our autumn feast is
not that of arrogant squirrels,
screaming banshees chattering in trees,
smuggling and hoarding spruce cones
in apex of branch, buried in hobbit holes of trunk.

It is not that of Indian River
after the fall salmon spawn
before completion of the dam,
but the grateful return to Blue Lake —
crystalline breath of glacier,

cut glass plates from grandmothers,
women before, frosted green carnival glass;
amber tumblers etched with deer
in the silence of snowy forest; lace
tablecloth, flicker of candle, the smooth
fold of linen napkins.

After the nash of flaked smoked salmon,
the savor of turkey, stuffed with crumbs
of sourdough bread, pecans, peridot of chunked
celery and diced butter clams from a nearby beach —
my sense this day is we all hold hands —
and in our fullness travel the coastline of gratitude:
for cold water, family, shared meal, and even squirrels.

My Daughter Teaches Me to Read a Poem

The stone in the stream.
Rock in the tide.

> *Mama, put a pen*
> *in your mouth*

Fixed in place, stone
and rock play the water's tune.

> *Bite down.*
> *Read around it.*

On a Sandbank in Willow Creek They Find Your Body

Were you fisherman traveler chasing
a summer run of pink salmon?

Did you tumble in head first, or collapse
into a short slide from cutbank to stream?

What journey have you taken
in the year you've been gone?

Did you drift in the current, jostled
from one braided stream to another?

Did you follow the vapor trails
patterning the sky?

Silt against bone, as you
wandered the river's edge,

tributaries, the slippery
grass-thickened patches, bluffing

of firm ground hidden,
were you suddenly made buoyant?

Rain Down the Mountain

We will miss him. Always had a smile on his face and a story to tell.

I. City building official and photographer

In Fishermen's Eye Gallery hangs a photo,
stretched canvas: Sitka rooftops viewed
through a second-story window, awash
in pelting rain. Rust and gray; waxwing
and herring gull.

II. City building official and pie taster

At the Backdoor Café tucked behind the bookstore,
Bernadette-who-loves-children serves organic jo,
pumpkin pie. He buys a slice for breakfast, chats
with our kindergartener as she hands back his change.

III. City building official and missing

When the bodies of the brothers are found, his wife
stands at the edge
of instability.
In garden gloves, she readies
to knuckle down;
move the mountain
by hand.

*Seven slides buckle
the mountain in frenzied rain;
crack, grumble, flicker.*

92

Sound

Between rain showers
I sneak out on the porch
at night to watch the outlined shadows
of my early spring plants
the foreground
setting for larger trees:
yellow cedar and spruce.
Soused with dew:
the step, the lawn.
A night ideal
for slug trekking
as they venture
through the yard,
picking up plant debris and
leaving slimy trails
that stick to the noses
of my dogs in the morning.
In the distance of this evening,
I hear the *"Om..."*
of mournful buoy
and I imagine its
black, cylindrical shape
bobbing in the sea
capturing the wind in its nook and crannies
chanting.
It makes me think of faraway places,
like China or Tibet
and monks.
There may be
a bit of these distant lands
found in Sitka Sound
not too far
from this porch.

Elegy

In memory of the poet Richard Dauenhauer.

Three weeks of drumming,
inches of rain in short hours. Mud sprints
into sea; salmon carcasses line the bank
in their return home to spawn.

A love song, this downpour:
Ravens, snow on the gunwales
of halibut boats in harbor,
moon skip across Flattop.

We don't count our days here, do we —
this rift in rain, this plummeting
sun, this candle, sun flash on sea,
your quiet residual voice?

At the Southern Entrance of Lynn Canal

Wind keens shrill, constant
through the ferry's forward lounge.
At Eldred Rock lighthouse,
snow collides and slides
the expanse of windows facing bow.

Snow drifts on deck.
It pools in the bulwark;
piles in the dark shadow
of rail, trunk and post;
it disappears into the nip of rough sea.

Time and again this
enters our story.
This howling wind, northern squall
long ago loneliness
illuminated by sound,
swallowed like tea.

New Moon

In its travel across sky
the slice of moon
spoons its darkened round
while the yellow dog
and black pup pair
in sleep by the stove.

Plates rattle in the kitchen.
Bruce drops a handful of hard noodles
into the boiling fury of stove-water:
bubble and sputter, we chatter
the absence of the crazy boss,
subtraction with our daughter,
the cold, lingering sun.

A kitchen silenced:
a constellation of family,
a darkened galaxy,
whispering stars and dust in orbit,
distant, without a sound.

Here we are,
forks full of noodles.
Stories tumbling around us,
take shape in their telling.
This one a star; another a pair
of sleeping dogs; still another
a hollowed crescent bowl.

48

You say, *I never thought my body*
would break down so soon.

Sun filters through green alder leaves,
breeze finds it way through an open window.

We are still, but for the quiet
moan of restless sleep.

Time snares even
this from us.

Elixir

A full martini, a toast to Monty
my daily drunk neighbor;
a tribute to living in the trailer
with the Chia Pet moss roof,
the back ass sliding,
sliding into the slow muddy creek behind it.

Lift a glass to Monty
for not running over my kid
after Happy Hour at the Moose
when he blasts up the cul-de-sac
in his shitty, serial killer van.

On warm May evenings,
Monty's music drifts like spruce pollen:
*Rhiannon rings like a bell through the night
and wouldn't you love to love her?*

What do you call beauty
in the darkness of addiction?

So cheers, Monty,
to booze that kills the pinprick
of living from one job's pay to another.
To booze that balms the working grind
of refrigeration, fiberglass, the bottle
that props you upright even when sober.

Querencia

At night
when the sky is pink
the neighbors eat yelloweye
and drink brown ale.

Through the open windows of my house and theirs
I hear there is huckleberry pie
for dessert, the bright fruit
picked from the bushes
between our homes.

And here, the lamp,
a glowing orb,
casts a fish eye of snug light,
on my empty desk.
Soon, autumn.

One word could fall
after another,
late summer catch,
stardust of thought.

Red berries crowd
the branch;
the sea, full
of snapper, sleeps
under the cosmos.

The Saltbox on Gibson Place

You'll know it by its purple doors, that house
built in the style of a modified saltbox.
Wind chimes slam dance from rusted nails,

tattered prayers tied in the hemlocks.
Come to the always-
open front door

breathe in the brine of the low tide air,
the view of Guide Island, the bipolar sea.
Step over the threshold; this is the heart

of my home: desk deluged
by runaway glass beads, rubber
and ink, my three favorite pens.

There are soft copies of *Winter News*,
Songs of the Pine Wife, rough
draft tanka, candle nubs.

This house offered retreat from jobs in the Arctic.
Two years we slept on the inflatable mattress, sat on the floor,
played Scrabble to bottles of Wild Horse and aged cheddar.

Baby on this floor, eyes shut
tight against sun, snow, and gale.
Robins — among the blades of wild iris.

Salmon heads drop from the sky in summer;
entrails in beak, eagles flapping by the window.
Brown bears stalking the trail behind our house,

their cubs trickling down the hill, rainwater
from the corner down spout.
Our neighbors

are fishermen, alcoholics;
they tend wild plots of fireweed.
They are routine in their inconsistencies.

Come for a visit, here
where the humpbacks yaw, here
between Vitskari Rocks and Kruzof Island.

About the Artist

Daphne Mennell has been a Yukon artist for over 37 years. Her inspiration comes from the many diverse and beautiful landscapes that make up the Yukon and Alaska. She has conveyed this love of nature and the wilderness in a number of mediums; various painting mediums as well as metal, silk and stone. *Full Moon on Windy Arm* is a painting in oils on canvas.

About the Author

Kersten Christianson is a raven-watching, moon-gazing, high school English-teaching Alaskan. She earned her MFA in Creative Writing/Poetry through the Low-Residency Program at the University of Alaska Anchorage in 2016. Her recent work has appeared in *Cirque, Tidal Echoes, San Pedro River Review, We'Moon, Sheila-Na-Gig* and *Pure Slush* among other literary journals. Kersten co-edits the quarterly journal *Alaska Women Speak.* When not exploring the summer lands and dark winter of the Yukon Territory, she lives in Sitka, Alaska with her husband and photographer Bruce Christianson, and daughter Rie.

Made in the USA
Columbia, SC
21 August 2017